**Bread**

# Read it together

This is a story about making bread, packed with lots of information — including a recipe. The humorous pictures show what fun cooking together can be!

Talking together about the book — the words and the pictures — gives children the chance to ask questions and understand the story better. It makes sharing books more enjoyable.

> Why does he put it somewhere warm?

> So the yeast can fill the bread with tiny bubbles of air.

> "I love making bread!"

> ... said Zed.

The repetition in this book makes it easy for young children to join in with the reading. This helps build their confidence and is part of learning to be a reader.

The labelled pictures of different breads at the back introduce children to one way that information can be set out in a book. Learning to read different kinds of books is important from the very early stages of reading.

Does that say doughnut?

How did you know that?

Can you show me where it says Zed?

When children have shared the book several times, you can draw their attention to repeated words, or letters from their name.

Zzz. There's Zed! Zzz. Like in pizza!

I love making pancakes! Can we?

If you keep the flour in the bowl!

Children often enjoy talking about a book after reading it. This gives them the chance to say what they liked best, and to talk about other books and experiences it reminds them of.

For Brita
with love, Mick

Distributed exclusively in Taiwan
for Hello! Book Club Inc

First published 2001 by Walker Books Ltd
87 Vauxhall Walk, London SE11 5HJ

2 4 6 8 10 9 7 5 3 1

Text © 2001 Mick Manning
Illustrations © 2001 Brita Granström
Introductory and concluding notes © 2001 CLPE/LB Southwark

This book has been typeset in Providence

Printed in Hong Kong

British Library Cataloguing in Publication Data:
a catalogue record for this book is
available from the British Library

ISBN 0-7445-6877-3

# Zed's Bread

written by **Mick Manning**

Illustrated by **Brita Granström**

**WALKER BOOKS**
AND SUBSIDIARIES

LONDON • BOSTON • SYDNEY

Zed was making some bread.
His little brother came to help.
Zed got out the bowl, spoon and jug,
and the flour, yeast, salt, oil and water.

"I love making bread!"
said Zed.

Zed mixed the ingredients into a dough.
He scooped and stirred them,
lifted and folded them.

"I love making bread!"
said Zed.

Zed left the dough in a warm place to rise.
It grew bigger and bigger,
fatter and fatter.

"I love making bread!"
said Zed.

Zed kneaded the dough on the floury table.
He punched and squashed it,
stretched and squeezed it.

"I love making bread!"
said Zed.

Zed made different shapes with the dough.
He rounded and patted it,
rolled and plaited it.

"I love making bread!"
said Zed.

Zed baked the bread in the oven.
It turned golden brown,
crispy and crunchy.

"I love making bread!"
said Zed.

Zed took the bread out of the oven.
It was crusty and hot,
and it smelt really good.

"I love making bread!"
said Zed.

Zed sliced two rolls.
He spread them with butter,
and sticky red jam.

"We love EATING bread!"
said Zed ... and Jed.

fried eggy bread

toast

Zed and Jed love bread!
They eat bread in lots of different ways.

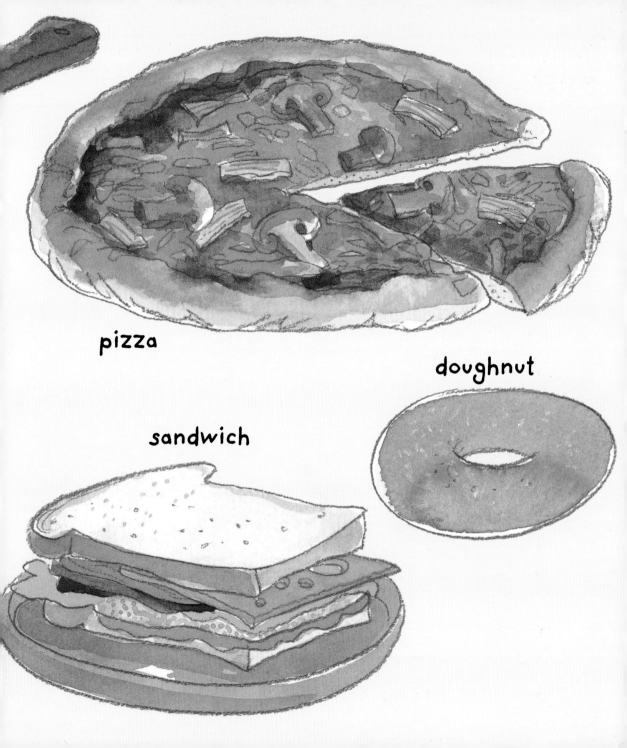

pizza

doughnut

sandwich

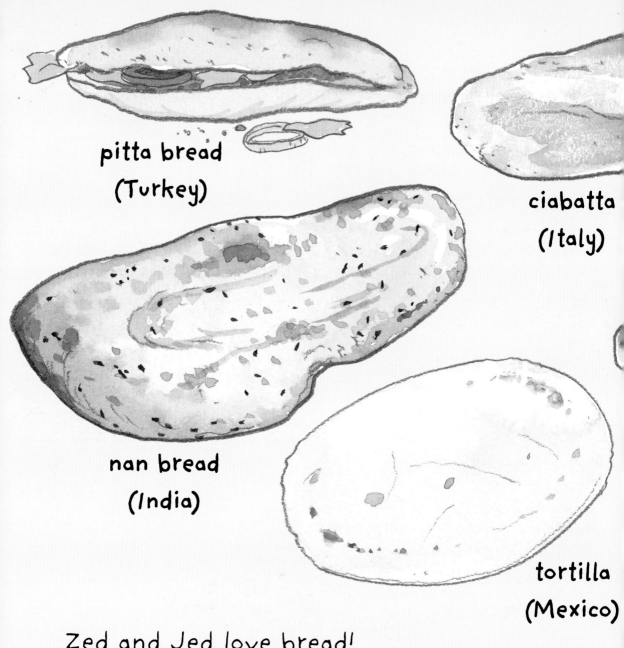

pitta bread
(Turkey)

ciabatta
(Italy)

nan bread
(India)

tortilla
(Mexico)

Zed and Jed love bread!
They eat bread from around the world.

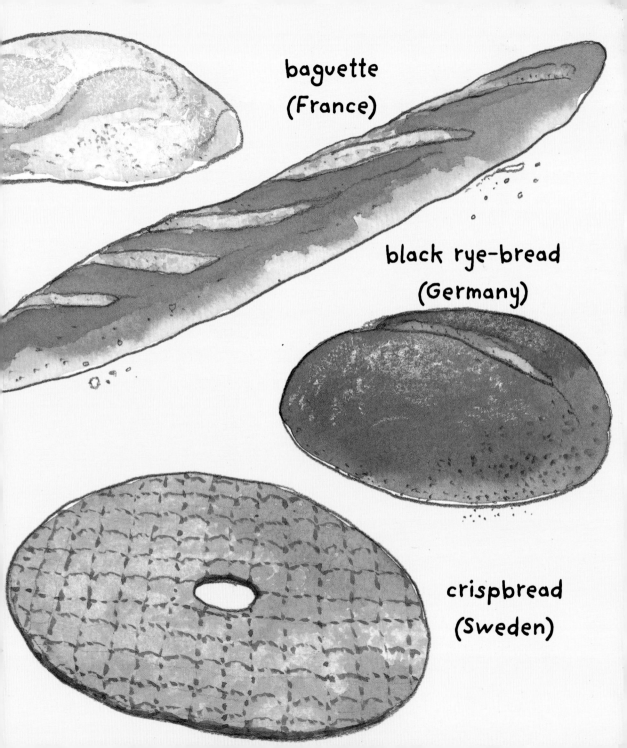

baguette
(France)

black rye-bread
(Germany)

crispbread
(Sweden)

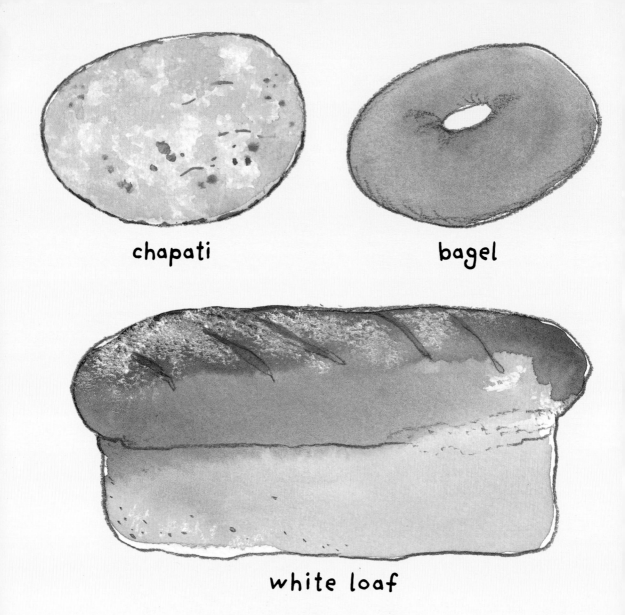

chapati

bagel

white loaf

Zed and Jed love bread!
They eat bread of different shapes and sizes.

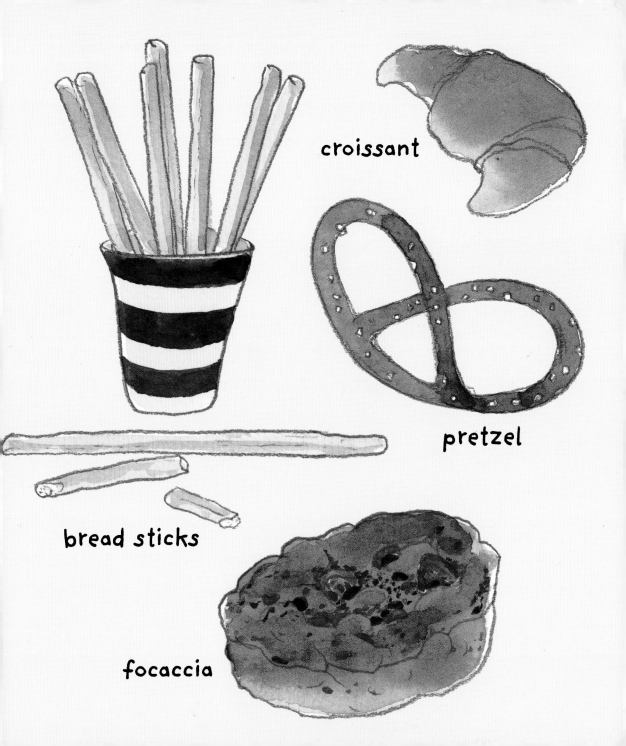

croissant

pretzel

bread sticks

focaccia

# Zed's Bread Recipe
## Makes 16 rolls

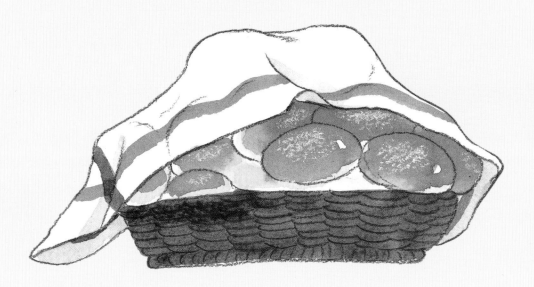

## You will need:

sieve
large mixing bowl
wooden spoon
measuring jug
greased baking tray
oven gloves

1 kg strong white bread flour
2 teaspoons salt
2 sachets dried yeast
550-600 ml lukewarm water
2 tablespoons sunflower oil
a little milk, for brushing

*Before you start cooking, remember to
wash your hands and put on an apron.*

Sieve the flour and the salt into the bowl. Mix in the dried yeast. Make a well in the centre and add the warm water and the oil. Stir them all together with the spoon and then use your hands to make the dough into a ball.

Put the dough on a floured surface. Knead it with your hands for about 10 minutes until it is smooth and elastic.

Put the dough back in the bowl and cover it with clingfilm. Leave it in a warm place for about an hour until it has doubled in size.

Knead it again on the floured surface for about 5 minutes.

Divide the dough into 16 pieces and shape them into bread rolls. You can make round rolls, plaits or twists — whatever you feel like.

Preheat the oven to Gas Mark 6 /200°C/400°F.

Put the rolls on the greased baking tray and leave them in a warm place for about 40 minutes to double in size. Then brush them lightly with milk and put them in the hot oven for 12–15 minutes until they are golden brown. Use oven gloves to take them out and leave them to cool on a wire rack — then they are ready to eat!

# Read it again

## Tell the story
Encourage children to tell the story about making bread in their own words. They can use the pictures in the book to remind them of the details.

*He squeezed it and punched it and put it in the bowl.*

## Dough letters
Using dough or modelling clay, encourage children to roll out letters in their name. They might like to make other letters from the alphabet, too. These can be baked and played with.

*Look, mummy, b is like d.*

## Act it out
Using a bowl and spoon children can act out the story, adding their own ideas and making up new endings.

*Now I'm going to put some water in.*

## Daily bread

Think together about all the bread you eat in a day. You could look in the kitchen and make a collection. Children can draw pictures of what they eat at different times and you can help label them.

## Picture story

The pictures tell a story that isn't written in the words. Talk with your child about what they see going on and encourage them to tell the story of Jed, Zed's baby brother.

## Make it, bake it!

Follow the recipe on the previous page and enjoy making and tasting your own bread.

# Reading Together

Reading Together Parents' Handbook
Myra Barrs and Sue Ellis

## Red Books 2-4 years

## Yellow Books 3-5 years

## Blue Books 4-6 years

## Green Books 5-7 years